A souvenir guide

Colby Woodland Garden

Pembrokeshire

Stephanie Mahon

National Trust

A Garden in a Coalfield

At first glance, Colby Woodland Garden appears to be a typically Welsh garden; a place of freedom and escape from the outside world, with diverse planting in its secluded, Pembrokeshire valley. Look beneath the surface, however, and the truth is sure to surprise you.

The Meadow with Colby Lodge in the distance

GARDD
GARDEN

CWM
VALLEY

MAES GLO
COALFIELD

COETIR
WOODLAND

MWYNGLODDIO
MINING

The Meadow, with its pretty wildflowers and babbling streams, seems as if it has always been there, serene and tranquil. It's hard to imagine this vista of natural beauty pockmarked by mine shafts and spoil heaps. Yet at the birth of the Colby Estate, it was this industrial landscape that would have been seen from the windows of the house. The woods, now a spiderweb of pathways and nature walks down to the coast, were not created as a refuge for people and wildlife, but rather as a money-making operation, managed for timber production.

Nowadays, with our modern sensibilities, we would be repelled by the idea of mining pits, slag heaps and a logging operation in our back gardens. Yet during the Industrial Revolution – a time of huge growth and technological change – this only showed how well one was doing.

Colby's fortunes could have altered once mining in the valley ceased, but its proximity to the sea made it an attractive holiday retreat. Since the mid-19th century, it was looked after by a series of owners, each adding their own touches. With the planting of exotic new trees and shrubs from the East, the beginnings of a garden emerged.

In the beginning

The Colby estate as we know it today is not an estate in any real sense, having been bought and sold, divided up, added to and resold many times over the centuries. It is, in fact, a diverse collection of properties, smallholdings and farms brought together at various different times, until the National Trust began to consolidate the land from 1980 onwards.

What we now consider the Colby Estate was originally known as the hamlet of Rhydlangoig or Rhydlancoed, meaning 'ford by the hollow bank' or 'ford of the wood'. Originally belonging to the nearby Kilgetty Estate, it was owned by Sir John Phillipps the younger during the 16th century. His son Richard Phillipps, who became Lord Milford, also had a part to play later in the Colby tale. Yet the real story begins in the mid 1700s, when Lady Phillipps sold off parcels of land from the estate after her husband's death in 1629.

Land for sale

Some of these parcels were bought by the Skyrmes. At first it seemed they would spend generations in the valley, but when his father William died in 1762, Thomas Skyrme was left to pay off considerable debts. His parents had taken out several mortgages, and his mother refused to pay the debts from her husband's business dealings. Thomas also had his own debts, owing the huge amount of £5,150 (just over £800,000 today). The High Court ordered their holdings to be sold, and the Skyrmes never achieved the heights to which they aspired.

The auction of '1,544 acres and three roods' took place in Haverfordwest on 5 September 1787, and one John Colby bought 50 hectares (123 acres) in three lots at a cost of £1,050 (close to £148,750 today). This is where the story of Colby Woodland Garden as we know it really begins.

Left Colby is known for its exotic displays of magnolias

John Colby and the Industrial Past

John Colby was born in 1751, on the cusp of an era of huge change. He studied law and joined the army, before inheriting his uncle Stephen's Ffynone estate in North Pembrokeshire in 1785.

This, it seems, was not enough for the ambitious new gentleman, who also had a house in Haverfordwest when he purchased the Skyrmes's land in 1787. However, he could not move in straight away. Documents dating from 1797 show that the purchase had still not been completed due to issues with the Skyrmes's debts. In 1800, when the matter was still not resolved, Colby's lawyer wrote to the agents to say he wasn't sure the sale was even valid. Another two years later, and Colby himself visited the agent at home in hope of forcing a settlement. It took a total of 15 years to gain possession of the land, and by this time he was already having a house built. It was called Colby Lodge and was completed in 1805.

It appears odd that John Colby should build another home when he already had a magnificent mansion at Ffynone, plus a town house in Haverfordwest. Lists of contents in the Lodge reveal there were only a few pieces of basic furniture, so it is doubtful that he or the family ever actually lived here.

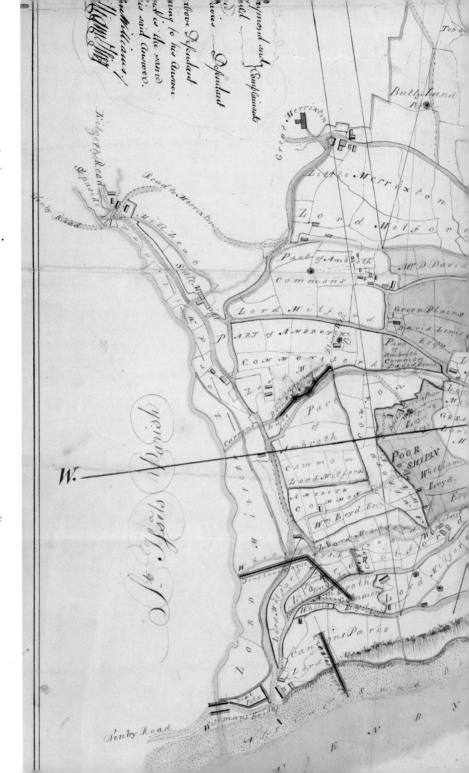

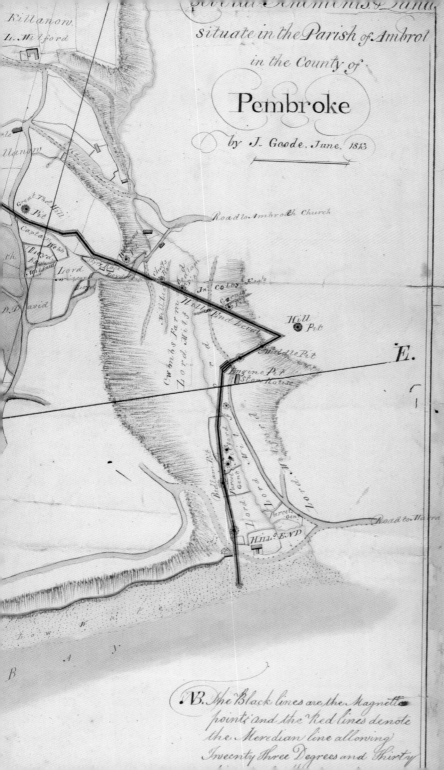

The answer may lie with Lord Milford, his friend and neighbour, with whom he shared military action and an interest in coal mining. The pair went 'sporting' – hunting with hounds – in the area, so it was well placed for resting on the occasional night or when travelling on business. This might be why it was called 'Lodge': to make clear its more rough-and-ready character, and to distinguish it from Colby House near Ffynone.

Left Goode's map of Pembrokeshire detailing the 'General Tenements & Land situated in the Parish of Amroth in the county of Pembroke', c. 1813

Nash up

After Colby inherited Ffynone, his family's country seat near Boncath, he commissioned up-and-coming architect John Nash to create a new house there. It is one of very few small mansions Nash designed during his early career, while he worked on several public buildings in Wales.

Given free rein by Colby to create whatever he wished at Ffynone, many believe this is where Nash first had the opportunity to develop and refine his own style. Nash's biographer describes it as 'the most successful of Nash's early houses … where we see for the first time … an original Nash interior.'

The property was passed down to John Vaughan Colby, who decided in 1901 to have the house remodelled and the gardens redesigned by Francis Inigo Thomas.

War in West Wales

John Colby was Lieutenant-Colonel Commandant of the Pembrokeshire Militia for 20 years, living through the Napoleonic Wars, as well as the last invasion of Britain.

The Battle of Fishguard

Colby was at his Haverfordwest house on the evening of 22 February 1797, when news broke that French troops had landed further up the coast near Fishguard. Colby sprang into action, assembling troops from anywhere he could, and sending word to Lord Milford at Picton Castle and Lord Cawdor at Stackpole.

He rode for Fishguard to find Thomas Knox, who led the town's voluntary infantry. Knox, like many officers of the landed gentry, had bought his commission and had no combat experience, but nonetheless seemed determined to engage the enemy. Colby was surprised to find only 70 men with Knox, who was bewildered by the invasion and slow to react.

Colby was even more alarmed when the clueless Knox divulged a plan to attack at dawn. He advised the young Knox to be content with a show of strength to hold the enemy in check. Colby was back in Haverfordwest by dawn, finding more men, and by noon he was marching north once more with 440 soldiers, sailors, volunteers and cavalry, and two cannons.

The British forces met outside Fishguard, and set up headquarters in the town – in what is now the Royal Oak pub. Colby's friend Lord Milford was the Lord Lieutenant and senior Captain of the Pembroke Yeoman Cavalry and the default man-in-charge. But the young Lord Cawdor persuaded Milford to hand over command. This was highly unusual, but neither Colby nor any of the other officers disputed it. Cawdor was a strong personality and is often given the credit for victory over the French; but it was John Colby who assembled the men for battle.

Above A contemporary illustration of the Battle of Fishguard entitled 'Carngwasted & Ebewalin' by James Baker, first published in Baker's *A Picturesque Guide to the Local Beauties in Wales, Vol II*, 1791

Opposite, top Welsh *Landscape with Two Women Knitting* by William Dyce, c. 1860. Apparently the French mistook the women's traditional dress as military uniforms, leading them to believe the British force was in the thousands

Opposite, below The monument commemorating the last invasion of Britain at Carreg Wastad Point, Pembrokeshire

Heroines amongst men

Even with this hasty rallying of troops, the British force was small, at most 750 against 1,400. It was only with the help of the civilian population that they prevailed. After a night of looting and drunken destruction on coastal farms by the infamous Légion Noire – a band of irregular convicts, republicans and deserters – the locals were hostile and keen to join in the fight.

One local cobbler, Jemima Nicholas, single-handedly rounded up 12 interlopers with a pitchfork and delivered them personally to town. She was awarded a pension of £50 a year for life and became a Welsh folk heroine, known ever after as 'Jemima the Great'.

At the time, many Welsh women wore the traditional dress of long red cloaks and tall black hats. On a misty February night, it would be hard to make out more than basic shapes and colours from afar, and the French mistook the attire for military uniforms, leading them to believe the British force was in the thousands.

Surrender before battle

Except for a few brief clashes, a couple of abandoned attack and ambush plans, and exaggerations on Cawdor's part about the size of his army, the 'Battle of Fishguard' never really took place. The entire debacle was over by dusk the next day, when the French offered an unconditional surrender. A tapestry entitled *The Last Invasion of Britain* was made to commemorate the battle, stitched by more than 70 women over a course of two years, and is now on display at Fishguard Library.

In the years following, Colby became obsessed by the thought of another invasion and gradually lost the respect of his dispirited militia. He sent them first to Ireland in 1799 and, following an uprising in Cork, asked his men to extend their service. They refused and tried to get him court-martialled. To save face, Colby handed over his command and resigned.

Men of means and mines

Newly free and idle, John Colby focused instead on building Colby Lodge and began mining in the area with Lord Milford.

He was also in charge of the collieries of his nephew, Sir Hugh Owen, the 6th baronet of Orielton. The Owens were a wealthy aristocratic family that Colby's sister Anne had married into, but there was no love lost between Colby and his brother-in-law Sir Hugh Owen, the 5th baronet, who considered him 'a conceited puppy'.

Little Hugh Owen was only four when his father died under mysterious circumstances, so Colby was free to run his ward's businesses, assuming control of considerable mining interests. He was once accused of embezzling money from his nephew's estates, but found not guilty. It was at this time Colby developed a hefty debt of £2,500, having to use his military fees to pay it off.

The Kilgetty Vein

The coastline from Amroth to Saundersfoot is peppered with old coal and ironstone mines. From the industrial archaeology that remains, we know there was small-scale bell-pit mining on the Colby Estate, which would only have supported a handful of miners. Yet papers and mining commissioners reports of the period show that Lord Milford mined Colby's land as well as his own, building adits, saw pits and winding houses, and taking water from the ponds and streams for his operations. Colby's accounts reveal he got one third of the profits from whatever Milford found on his land, for no outlay – a sweet deal in anyone's books.

The main product of these mines was anthracite – a top-ranking coal, as it burnt hot without much smoke. It was used by Queen Victoria on the Royal Yacht and was in great demand. Pembrokeshire produced the highest-quality anthracite, and so Milford and Colby believed they would strike gold with the Kilgetty Vein; it was 95 percent pure carbon and the only workable anthracite seam in the area. With the seam only 18–21 in (45–53 cm) thick, miners had to lie on their sides using a shovel and pick to extract the coal.

Left The southern edge of Colby Estate at Amroth beach. The mined coal would be taken via the Wiseman's Bridge road, then through tunnels in the cliffs to Saundersfoot harbour

Opposite, top A contemporary illustration of a girl putter down the mines

Opposite, below There were inspections for the conditions of child labourers throughout the 19th century

'I have been down bout three years. When I first went down I couldn't keep my eyes open. I don't fall asleep now. I smokes my pipe: smokes half a quarter a week.'

William Richards, aged 7, quoted in a mining commissoner's report, 1840

Life in the mines

It was not just men undertaking this gruelling labour. During the 19th century, it was customary for whole families to work down the mines, including women and children. It was harsh work, with boys and girls as young as five earning their keep by crawling on all fours and hauling tubs of coal underground; or dragging trams weighing a quarter of a tonne, barefoot, with just a candle fixed to their caps to light the darkness. Ailments such as spinal and pelvic distortions were common, as were bleeding feet with boils, asthma and bronchitis. A mining commissoner's report published in 1840 concluded that: 'anyone can distinguish a collier's child from the children of other working people.' These children worked longer hours than their elders – seven days a week – and they could not expect to live past 40. Indeed, life was brutal for the rural folk of West Wales during the Victorian era. People lived hand to mouth in dire conditions, in houses with mud floors and no furniture. A reporter for *The Times* in 1843 describes labourers' cottages in Haverfordwest as 'mud hovels' with 'nothing but loose straw and filthy rugs' for beds: 'never did I witness such abject and wretched poverty.' Evictions and starvation were commonplace, and many died from diseases including cholera, typhoid, dysentery and tuberculosis. Living was simply about surviving.

Murder in the woods: the Mary Prout case

'If they hang me, I'll tell the truth. I threw it in, and ran away a short distance, and then returned and found there was no noise'

Mary Prout to a local policeman on being arrested, 1864

It was into this grim world that the unfortunate Mary Prout was born, on 12 January 1843, to a family of miners in Amroth. The fifth child of ten, Mary tended the animals on the family's smallholding, taking occasional work in a lodging house in nearby Tenby. Described as 5ft 2ins tall, with a fresh complexion, brown hair and grey eyes, she was known as quiet, simple, good-natured girl.

When Mary turned 18, her mother died and her father remarried less than two years later. His new wife Ann did not take to her stepdaughter. She no doubt saw Mary as just another mouth to feed, and felt that at her age she should already be married off. Soon after her father's marriage, Mary was caught stealing money from a greengrocer, for which she was sentenced to six weeks' hard labour. There was no warm welcome upon returning home with a conviction and, to make matters worse, within a month Mary had fallen pregnant.

Out of wedlock

The unnamed father was nowhere to be seen, so she carried the stigma of having a child out of wedlock alone - the highest form of shame for a woman in Victorian Britain. She was admitted to the dreaded local workhouse in Narberth and gave birth to her daughter, Rhoda, on 9 April 1864. Mary was an affectionate mother and fond of her baby. On visiting home briefly after the birth to collect some clothes, she was told not to return with an illegitimate child.

Six weeks after Rhoda was born, mother and baby were released from the workhouse. Left to fend for themselves, they had no money, food, support or income. In desperation, Mary made the long walk back to her grandmother's house with babe in arms, and on the way meeting two local women near the Colby Estate at around 8pm. Yet Mary's grandmother stated that she arrived home only half an hour later, alone, agitated and crying, saying the child had died in the workhouse.

Suspicion was aroused the next day, when rumours of the two conflicting stories got round. A search began and, deep within Colby's West Wood at the bottom of Chart's pit, the body of a child was found with a fractured skull. Mary was arrested the following morning, and the policeman recalled her raving: 'if they hang me, I'll tell the truth. I threw it in, and ran away a short distance, and then returned and found there was no noise.'

GLOWYR
MINERS

TRYCHINEB
TRAGEDY

LLOFRUDDIAETH
MURDER

TLOTY
WORKHOUSE

DIGARTREF
HOMELESS

MAM
MOTHER

On trial

At her trial Mary pleaded not guilty. A string of witnesses testified for the prosecution, and the defence tried to build a case that madness ran in the family: citing two of Mary's great aunts who would frequently strip naked in public, and another who died in a lunatic asylum. The jury found her guilty of 'wilful murder' but recommended mercy on the grounds that there was no premeditation. The judge sentenced her to hang, to gasps from the court, and Mary was removed crying and moaning.

The case resulted in widespread sympathy for Mary. The Reverend W. D. Phillips, Vicar of Amroth, who had baptised Mary as a child, instigated a plea for clemency to the Queen. Just five days after the trial, Mary's sentence was commuted to 20 years' imprisonment – a remarkably fast turnaround. Although this could have merely out of sympathy for Mary's plight, many believe it was something more; an indication that Rhoda's unknown father was in fact a man of influence.

Remembering Mary

Mary served 14 years in various London prisons, and was released on the anniversary of the day she was arrested. She returned to Pembrokeshire and worked in Saundersfoot as a housekeeper for local farmer James Rees, a widower 20 years her senior. They later married and had two children, John and Mary, who eventually left home and worked in London as a waiter and waitress. Mary Prout lived until 1921, and died in London, no doubt to be nearer her children. You can see her gravestone at St Elidyr's churchyard in Amroth, erected by her loving son and daughter with the inscription: 'Dear mother, rest, thy work is o'er. Thy loving hands shall toil no more. No more thy gentle eyes shall weep. Rest, dear Mother, gently sleep. Erected by her sorrowing children.'

As for her baby daughter, Rhoda, she is buried in the same graveyard as her mother, in an unmarked grave.

Right Millbank prison, London where Mary was sent after her trial

The 'Bastardy Clause'
One of the most controversial features of the 1834 Poor Law Amendment Act was the 'Bastardy Clause'. With the aim of preventing extra-marital pregnancy and restoring female morals, the law made mothers solely responsible for any illegitimate children unless they could prove paternity. Unable to support themselves and their offspring, desperate mothers would enter the parish workhouse as a last resort. Census figures of 1851 reveal that a third of inmates at Narberth workhouse were bastard children, and by 1861 this had increased to more than 50 per cent.

The new law caused widespread debate. Mary Prout's neighbour, when giving evidence in a parliamentary inquiry into the Rebecca Riots in 1843 *(see page 21)*, argued against the injustices of the Act, stating: 'I think in nine cases out of ten, during the old law, they married; and I think in thirteen cases out of fifteen, they [the young men] do not marry now.' It was not until 1872 that the law was changed so that fathers once again shared parental responsibility.

Creation of the Garden

After almost a century of mining at Colby, the last pits closed in 1843 and the house was eventually sold off. In the years following, a series of new owners put their mark on the place – adding exotic plants and reworking the old mine tracks – and the beginnings of a garden emerged.

Closing of the mines

At the ripe old age of 60, John Colby married his cousin Cordelia, and proceeded to have nine children. Upon his death in 1823, his son, also John Colby, inherited Colby Lodge and its land, but showed little interest in the property. The coal had run out quickly, with little profit, and in 1843 he placed an advertisement in the local paper letting the house.

The Kays

Tenants came and went, including a dental surgeon called Thomas Evans, who offered 'water treatments' in a 'hydropathic establishment' where 'patients may be treated mesmerically'. Everything changed in 1873, however, when Major Samuel Kay and his wife Sarah, from Stockport, bought Colby Lodge at auction as a holiday home. A chemist, Kay set up 'Kay Brothers' firm with his brother, Thomas. Together they developed products such as transparent cement for fixing broken china and glass, as well as manufacturing goods used in the First World War; everything from 'sticky bombs' to packaging for Mepacrine – a newly discovered anti-malaria drug. The brothers' fortune was made selling 'Kay's Compound Essence of Linseed', a popular gargle mixture for coughs and colds. In 1884 they received a royal warrant as chemists to Queen Victoria.

Above The Croslands reworked old mining tracks into footpaths, such as this one in the West Wood

Left A budding magnolia in early spring

Opposite A map planning out the pathways and irrigation systems of the Woodland Garden, c. 1934

Land for leisure

Thomas Kay travelled extensively around the world, and would return home with gifts from far-flung places for his brother's estate. These included exciting new plants from the Himalayas such as magnolias, rhododendrons and azaleas, which Samuel planted in the woods, in the hopes of developing an exotic arboretum.

The Kays reworked old mining tracks as garden paths, and employed seven gardeners to look after the estate, including the woodland, walled kitchen garden and a more formal garden around the house. John Colby's generation had used their estates to generate wealth, but at the turn of the 19th century, being truly well-off meant having land just for leisure. Creating a garden for pleasure filled with expensive plants was the ultimate expression of how rich and well-connected you were, and the upwardly mobile Kays were no exception.

The Croslands

Samuel's daughter Gladys was a passionate gardener. Upon inheriting the estate after the First World War, she moved to Colby with her husband, Lieutenant Colonel James Crosland. Together they redesigned the gardens, adding many rare varieties of hydrangea, and installing an irrigation system to make sure these precious specimens survived It was managed by a few gardeners, supplemented occasionally by extra hands such as Italian prisoners of war. The couple also bred pheasants, which would wander about the grounds, and created the trout pond in the meadow.

Gladys's generosity was borne out by her many donations to St Elidyrs Church in Amroth, including paying to have its bells recast. But a tale recounted by one of her workers shows Gladys in rather a different light: when her husband was working in the field and suddenly dropped dead, the workers were told to 'keep on, and get the hay in!'

'[She] delighted in showing people through the woods, which were beautifully landscaped. She did a lot of gardening herself and it was a common sight to see her gardening in apron and gloves among her beloved rhododendrons.'

A friend of Mrs Crosland

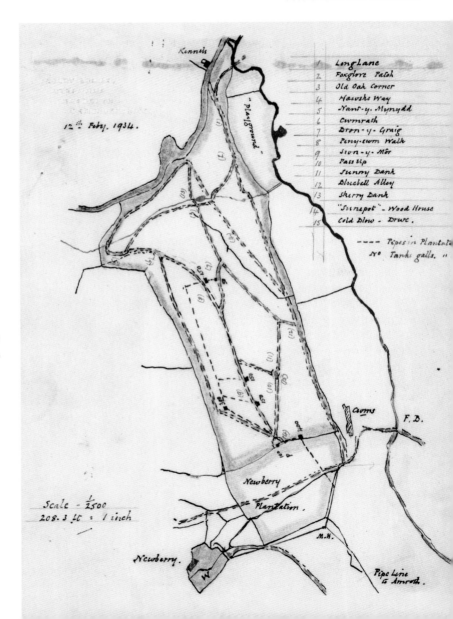

The post-war years

On Mrs Crosland's death in 1950, the Colby Estate of nearly 900 acres (364 hectares) passed to her niece, Miss Elidyr Florence Dixon Mason. Independently wealthy, Miss Mason never married, choosing instead to invest in flashy cars and revelling in doing as she pleased.

There was a little cottage known as Brookside on her land, which captivated any who walked by. Miss Mason got so annoyed with people asking to rent it that she had it knocked down. She did not take to living in the big, old house, and instead had a modern bungalow built on the western side of the valley. In 1965, she sold Colby Lodge and over 16 acres to Peter and Pamela Chance, including the Walled Garden, the East Wood and the Meadow.

Miss Mason and Pamela worked together over the years to beautify the woodland, and it was clear Miss Mason loved the trees a great deal. According to a gardener, when Peter Chance once asked her to fell an enormous old beech tree that was becoming dangerous, she conceded, but cried as it was being taken down. Miss Mason died in 1979 – worth, some say, more than £1 million – and bequeathed her 356 hectares (880 acres) at Colby to the National Trust.

Right   A photograph of
Colby Lodge in 1963

By Chance

The new owners of Colby Lodge, meanwhile, had put their mark on the place, with a charming Victorian Gothic gazebo in the Walled Garden, and a selection of statuary, urns, fountains and gates.

Ivan Oswald Chance, who called himself Peter, was best known as chairman of Christie's Auction House, and was often seen on television selling famous works of art. He and Pamela used Colby as a weekend home, and would invite visitors such as his childhood nanny down to stay for the holidays.

During their time, there was a croquet lawn in the Meadow, until the moles got in, and two rescue donkeys called Minnie and Joseph. Fruit and vegetables grown on site were sent up to London on the train each week, and unusual shrubs and climbers arrived by the truckload to add to a growing collection of treasures, including old-fashioned roses.

Peter died in 1984, having transferred the property to the National Trust. The organisation then bought back other original farms and woods in the area, with grant aid from the Countryside Commission, creating the estate as we see it today.

Above The Chances commissioned the gazebo in the 1970s

Top left A photograph of Peter and Pamela Chance in their early seventies

Top right When the Scourfield-Lewises took on the restoration of the Walled Garden in the 1980s, they used the concrete beds for ornamental planting and made the Gazebo the focal point of the space

Restoring the Walled Garden

The basic Lodge interior was of little historic interest, so the Trust leased the house to Cynthia and Tony Scourfield-Lewis, asking them to also take on the Walled Garden. Not only did they take on this huge restoration project, but kindly agreed to 'open it to the public on every day that the Woodland Garden was also open', along with another section of the private garden to the west of the house (an arrangement that the current occupants of the Lodge have kindly continued). In 1986, the couple began work, transforming what had been an overgrown kitchen garden into a formal pleasure garden, adding a pool, rill and various beds and borders. They left the grid of concrete raised – or coffin – beds, but used them for ornamental not edible plants, and made the Chances' gazebo the focal point of the whole space.

In 2010, guardianship of the Walled Garden reverted back to the National Trust. The garden team began implementing plans to boost year-round interest by adding more colourful seasonally flowering perennials and shrubs to make the most of the Scourfield Lewises' years of hard work. Cynthia passed away in 2013, and a sculpture dedicated to her memory called *Nurture* sits just to the left of the entrance to the Walled Garden.

Exploring Colby

Colby Woodland Garden has been brought together, separated and reunited by various owners at various different times, and all with wildly different tastes. The result is a quirky patchwork of diverse and colourful spaces with unusual and quixotically placed sculptural elements; a garden of discovery for everyone who visits.

A hidden valley

Visitors can relax in the calm surroundings of the Walled Garden with its floriferous borders, or figure out the optical illusions in its intriguing Gazebo. Younger visitors can enjoy running free in the Meadow, watching the bees and butterflies dancing on the wildflowers, racing rubber ducks in the stream, or take it turns on the rope swings and log bridges.

In the shady hush of the woods, there are secret spaces to explore and fascinating features to find. Dotted here and there among the trees are traces of the garden's mining past, and the prized rhododendrons give a magnificent display of colour in springtime. Those who are more eagle-eyed might spot a bird of prey gliding silently overhead, glimpse a dipper flitting along the stream, or spot one of the little brown trout rising to feed on the abundant insect life hatching from the surface of the water.

Then beyond all this lies the sea, beautiful coastal views and a sandy beach that reveals its own mysteries at low tide.

GLÖYNNOD BYW
BUTTERFLIES

GWANWYN
SPRING

ADAR
BIRDS

PLANNU
PLANTING

COED
TREES

BORDERI
BORDERS

The Walled Garden

It is not known exactly when Colby's Walled Garden was first created. Sheltered gardens such as this, laid out on a grid plan for growing vegetables, were typical of the Victorian period; so it's possible it was built by the Kays.

The garden is sloped, protected from the coastal winds and salt by the woodlands as well as the high, stone walls. It features deep raised beds, known as 'coffin' beds, which offer a greater depth of soil for edible crops. Since the 19th century, kitchen gardens such as this would have been used to grow all manner of vegetables and orchard fruit; with the addition of a glasshouse, it would also have been possible to cultivate more tender fruits such as peaches and plums.

Although its early life was dedicated to produce, the garden as we see it now is a formal incarnation of ornamental planting and carefully curated features; a pleasure garden with climbers growing up the walls, fine trees, interesting shrubs and borders full of eye-catching flowers.

The Gazebo
Upon walking through the gate and up the steps, the first thing you notice is the gazebo at the top of the garden. Commissioned by the Chances in the 1970s, this octagonal summerhouse was designed by the local architect Wyn Jones. The charming exterior is reminiscent of the Victorian Gothic style, but it is the trompe-l'oeil paintings on the interior that make it really special.

Created freehand by a young American artist called Lincoln Taber, their life-like quality makes it difficult to tell the difference between what is real and what is not. A note pinned to the wall, a key hanging on a hook, a lily in a glass vase – these delightful details were designed to fool the eye.

On the ceiling are illustrations of the zodiac signs, relating to the eight people involved in its construction. The Gazebo is equipped with underfloor heating and a mini kitchen hidden in two built-in cupboards. On the back wall, Taber painted the view he saw looking out from inside as he was working – giving a glimpse of what the view down the garden might have been like in 1975.

Ornamental planting

The same view is now quite different, taking in a 'cascade' or rill that flows down to a circular pool created by Tony and Cynthia Scourfield-Lewis. Alongside is a rockery of alpine plants and lawn punctuated with island beds. The grid of raised planters, once home to vegetables and herbs, now features topiary yew pyramids, and flowers in spring and summer.

The Scourfield-Lewises added many new areas to the space, such as the hebe walk and fuchsia garden, shrubbery, magnolia corner, rose bed, mahonia border and informal orchard. They also introduced some pieces of contemporary sculpture, although it was the Chances before them who brought in the lead urns, the cherub and the cistern by the gate.

Opposite, top The realistic trompe l'oeil paintings by Lincoln Taber inside the Gazebo are designed to fool the eye

Opposite, below The Scourfield-Lewises added many pieces of contemporary sculpture into the Walled Garden

Top right The sun sets over the Walled Garden in June

Slug control quacked
Everything at Colby is managed in as bio-friendly a way as possible, to encourage wildlife, including chemical-free methods to control pests and diseases. As a result, the garden team has come up with innovative ways to keep down the populations of snails and slugs, who like to munch on the precious plants in the walled garden. The solution: three resident Colby ducks, who roam the beds and borders in search of tasty mollusc morsels.

The Meadow

Opposite The Meadow is
full of wildflowers in the
high summer

Opposite right The ponds
at the bottom of the
Meadow

The open ground of four acres in front of Colby Lodge and between the two woodlands is a flood meadow, which is managed for wildlife.

Each spring and summer, the grass is allowed to grow tall, creating an abundant wildflower display that attracts bees, butterflies and other key pollinators. In late summer, after the wildflowers have had their chance to set seed, it is cut down and the hay removed to help reduce the soil fertility; this gives the wildflowers a better chance to compete with the grasses. The edges of the Meadow are important feeding grounds for bats; they need the shelter of the trees, but love to feed on the flying insects emerging from the streams and ponds, as well as from amongst the grasses and wildflowers.

The stream that runs through the Meadow is clean and clear, and full of trout – which also feed on the bounty of insects. There are several bridges that cross the water, and some stepping-stones for the risk-takers. On the east side, there are ample opportunities for natural play, including fallen tree trunks that beg to be climbed, rope swings and shallow pools in the stream.

BLODAU GWYLLT
WILDFLOWERS

BYWYD GWYLLT
WILDLIFE

PYLLAU
PONDS

GWEIRIAU
GRASSES

The ponds

Following the stream to the very bottom takes you to the most secluded area; where the trees meet the Meadow. Here you will find pathways weaving in and out of a small series of ponds. In spring, these ponds are home to clouds of wriggling tadpoles. On warm, late-summer evenings, damselflies and dragonflies fill the air with darting colour.

The Bedlam Pit

In the centre of the Meadow, you might spot a large mound – the remains of the Bedlam Pit from the days of John Colby's mining operations. Like many of the pits and shafts on the estate, this was once open, with ash trees planted around it, but there were developing concerns about safety. Peter Chance had the trees cut down, and the stumps pushed into the mine, which was then filled with soil from the pit's old spoil heaps.

Gatecrashers

At the entrance to the West Wood stand two cast-iron posts, which are all that remains of the old Kilanow toll gate. These 'gates' were used on highways all over Britain in the 19th century, to levy a fee or tax on all who wished to pass.

They became highly unpopular with poverty-stricken tenant farmers, particularly in South and West Wales. In May 1839, rioters with ash-smeared faces attacked the toll gates at Yr Efail Wen in Carmarthenshire. The riots flared up again in 1842, with many gates being broken and others set alight. They became known as the 'Rebecca Riots', due to the women's clothes the rioters wore to disguise their identities, and the chant they would perform beforehand.

There was no immediate visible effect after the riots ended, but in 1844 a new Turnpike Act was created that lowered the tolls. By the early 1900s, most of these gates had been shut down.

The East Wood

A walk in the East Wood begins in palatial style, through the grand gates placed at the entrance by Peter Chance.

The gates are said to be from Sion House in Tenby, which burned down in 1938. Built in 1790 and designed by John Nash, it was once the most prestigious development in town. It was also the reason for the last duel in Britain – in 1839 between Henry Mannix and William Richards, over a driveway dispute. Given its history, Peter Chance told his gardener he simply must have the gates in the garden.

Into the forest

Ascending the path, the shade of the canopy deepens and you enter the mystical woodland through a fern-lined gully. Listen closely and you may hear its inhabitants, including woodpeckers, owls, bats and badgers. Almost half of Colby's woodland is native oak, and the most species-rich habitat in the country. In the East Wood, there is a growing collection of Japanese maples, including some very unusual varieties. The Kew Millennium Seed Bank at Wakehurst often collects seed from a hidden grove of the rare chequer tree, *Sorbus torminalis*, which gives the prime minister's official country residence its name.

The plant destroyer

Some newer plantings have replaced trees that became infected with a rampant fungal disease called *Phytophthora* (which translates from Greek as 'the plant destroyer'). This nasty pathogen can strike down a vast array of plants and spreads easily through spores. It cannot be cured and so must be managed by felling and burning. The damp warm climate at Colby doesn't help matters, but the garden team is trying to halt its progress by planting resistant cultivars.

Above The fern-lined footpath that leads you into the woodland

Left Woodpeckers are one of the many birds that you can find in the East Wood

Opposite right A detail of the Peter Chance memorial. The carved symbol is made up two 'P's for Peter and Pamela

Opposite bottom Coins placed in the Penny Tree

The couple's memorials

As well as the trees, there are many other special features to discover in East Wood. The Peter Chance Memorial is a commanding sight; an obelisk that stands looking across the valley towards the memorial for his wife, Pamela. Those who knew them say they would often be working in different parts of the woodland, and call across the valley to each other. The couple had a fondness for repurposing old items – look closely and you might spot a section of a ship's mast 'planted' near the lower gates and a large stone urn nearby.

Industrial remains

Coming back down to the lane that runs beside the Meadow, visitors can add spare coins to the Penny Tree, started by Colby gardener Geraint and his children after a visit to the famous one at Lydford Gorge, Devon. A little farther along is the old Saw Pit used in the mines, like a slice cut out of the ground, lined with stone walls. This is where the timber from the woods would have been prepared for pit props and other uses – the 'top-dog' above guiding the cut and the 'under-dog' below providing the power, with a long-hand saw between them.

This space is littered with other reminders of Colby's industrial past. Old estate maps show this is where the winding house for lifting coal to the surface stood. The path was once the main carriageway to the Lodge and also the roadway that took the coal down to the beach to be loaded on to ships. Many accounts tell us that the vast majority of coal from Pembrokeshire pits was shipped by boats, with very little was taken inland – the roads in the county were so poor that heavily laden wagons struggled to make progress.

The West Wood

On the opposite side of the Meadow, the West Wood has just as many exciting sights to see. Towering beside the newt pond is an impressive Japanese redwood. This giant, which reaches well over 134m (440ft), is one of the tallest in the UK.

Spectacular scenery

Walking along the winding paths to the top of West Wood can be a steep climb, but well worth the effort. Sky-high views of the sea between Amroth and Carmarthen Bay can be had and, on a clear day, Worm's Head at the Gower Peninsular revealed in the distance. Within the woodland the scenery is similarly spectacular, with an abundance of seasonal and ornamental planting lighting the way. The rhododendrons and azaleas, which thrive in the valley's acidic soil, come into bright and beautiful bloom in May and June, filling the pathways with colour. As well as these are swathes of bluebells colonising the slopes and in late summer the large collection of hydrangeas come into flower. Glades of beech, plane, pine, and yew trees create spaces of a very different character altogether.

The curving pipe sticking out of the ground at the very top of the West Wood is part of the Crosland's irrigation system from the 1930s. A hydraulic ram pump in the valley below filled a series of pipes and galvanised tanks, where gardeners could refill their watering cans.

Right The giant Japanese redwood in West Wood

Right The Pamela
Chance Memorial

Below The winding
footpath at the top
of the West Wood

Pamela's memorial

Down on Long Lane is the Pamela Chance
Memorial, erected by Peter after her death in
1979. It is believed the seven pillars came from
Stackpole, on Lord Cawdor's estate further
west, while the cobbles cemented into the
centre came from Amroth beach. Peter intended
to add a canopy, but a failed attempt to remove
and use an old bandstand's roof was never
followed up.

Tales from the pit

Next to the path at the bottom of the West Wood
is a capped mine believed to be Chart's Pit, where
little Rhoda Prout was found (see page 10). It is
now closed off and fenced with planting around
it, but back in the Croslands' era it was still open,
and the site of another unfortunate incident.
Thieves had lain in wait in the woods until after
dark, before taking their opportunity to steal
some of the statues and garden features from the
grounds. Having dragged their heavy booty as
far as the West Wood, they were spooked by
something and, fearing capture, they decided to
get rid of the evidence quickly, dropping the
pieces down the shaft.

Wheel of fortune

Beside Chart's Pit is an iron wheel, which
remains somewhat of a mystery. Local
historians think it was once part of a drum
wheel used in the mines to hoist coal skips up
from the pithead. An empty skip, attached to
the drum with ropes, would be weighted with
water to lower it into the pit, where it was
then emptied and filled with coal. A second
skip at the top was then filled with water as a
counterweight to lift the coal to the surface.

Another theory was that it was once part of
a circular stone-saw mechanism driven by
water power, allegedly used by the
stonemason Henry Rees in the late 1700s,
who ran his stoneworks at Cwms cottage,
near the bottom of the Meadow. Yet when
similar wheel was found at a North Wales slate
quarry, it was generally accepted that, like the
North Wales quarry wheel, the wheel at Colby
formed one end of a drum, joined by staves to
a similar wheel.

Colby's Buildings

Colby Lodge

There may have been a farmhouse on the site of Colby Lodge in the 18th century, but it is doubtful it was a large residence. The Lodge was built between 1802–5 in the Georgian style, with strong, clean lines and large sash windows, but little embellishment. This was probably because of its status as an occasional residence or hunting lodge, which would naturally be more modest in decoration and comfort.

As John Colby employed John Nash to design his mansion at Ffynone, it was believed that Colby Lodge might also have been the work of Nash. However, there is no evidence of this, and was more likely the work of Mr George, Nash's clerk of works, who copied the Nash style and supervised the construction. The Lodge remains in private hands, so the garden immediately around the house is not open to visitors. Yet the fantastic displays of azaleas in spring, and Japanese maples in autumn, provide a delightful 'borrowed view' from the Pamela Chance Memorial.

The Kennels

Close to where the top of the Meadow and the West Wood meet, there is a charming miniature stone-built house. Too small for adults, it appears at first, with its cute little windows and door, as if it could be a most magnificent kid's playhouse.

This tiny cottage is, however, thought to have been the kennels for John Colby's hunting pack – a rather splendid place for his hounds to live. The chimneys once lead to fireplaces inside; probably not to pamper his pooches, but rather for the young worker who would have lived with and cared for the dogs. The remains of the walled dog yard can still be traced behind the building.

Outbuildings

Upon entering the garden from the car park there is a small cabin. Originally the engine house for the electricity generator, before the Lodge ran on mains power, it is now used as the National Trust shop. Likewise, the old stables are now The Bothy Tearooms (not National Trust) while the bothy was once the coach or carriage house. What is now the visitor toilets was once the garage, where Miss Mason kept her fast cars.

Farther down, across from the entrance to the Walled Garden, is a small building known as the Bat Shed (not open to visitors). This is a popular breeding roost for lesser horseshoe bats, among others. When the Trust took over the garden and began to investigate the property, a member of staff opened the shed and discovered enormous stacks of empty glass bottles, with separate piles for champagne, whiskey, and gin (among others). The Chances were social butterflies. Peter was known to be a wine connoisseur – when his wine collection was sold it fetched thousands of pounds. The bottles remain *in situ*, to avoid disturbing the bats, and so have been preserved for posterity, along with a large amount of bat guano.

Opposite, top   Colby Lodge has been on the estate since early 19th century, and remains a private residence

Left   The bothy next to the Bothy Tearoom in the courtyard used to be the Lodge's coach house

Top left   Piles of glass bottles, once belonging to Peter Chance, inside the shed behind the Lodge (not open to visitors)

Above   The Kennels, once home to John Colby's hunting dogs

Cottages and farmhouses

Little Craig-y-Borion

In 2014 it was decided to look again at the ruined farmhouse of Little Craig-y-Borion, hidden away in the middle of the estate, to see if it could be saved. The roof was still in place but would not last the winter. Both end walls had significant cracks and were falling away, so it was decided first to do an emergency rebuild. The following year the rest of the cottage was restored and equipped as an eco-house, with its own borehole for water. The central heating and hot water are powered by solar panels in summer and stoves in winter, fuelled by wood from wind-felled trees in the woodland.

Work in progress

The house is now used as a home for residential volunteers and working holiday groups. With all these extra hands on site, the amount of conservation work done at Colby has greatly increased; from reclaiming long-neglected areas of the garden, to developing the surrounding woods and farmland for nature conservation and public access.

A kitchen garden has been developed among the old outbuildings, to provide fresh produce for guests. An orchard of rare and ancient Welsh apple varieties has also been planted behind the cottage, along with an ever-increasing number of fruit bushes, to be used for jam and cider-making once mature.

A farming history

The history of the building has been traced back to the census records of 1793, when the 'tenants in common' of Little Craig-y-Borion were William Probyn of Newland, Gloucestershire, and Edward Thomas of Pilcoggan. Many local residents still remember the building when it was a working farm, recalling stories of the hard-working lives lived there, and have delighted in seeing it restored today.

Rose Cottage

Rose Cottage looks like a modern, single-storey house across the road that runs behind Colby Lodge, but is in fact an extension of a much smaller, older cottage. It has a charming garden with patio and lawn, and a stream running through it. Inside there is an open fireplace to keep you cosy after a day's walk around the woods and beach and it has a charming garden of its own, lovingly restored and cared for by volunteer David Weaver.

Little Breck

Little Breck is the bungalow Miss Mason had built for herself in 1964. Situated above the Woodland Garden, its quietly secluded location offers glimpses down the valley towards Amroth, from what is now a woodland glade garden. When Miss Mason built the house, the area was more of an open heathland ('breck' being an old word for heath), with views as far as the sea. The house has three bedrooms, a wood-burning stove and a set of Sixties-era servants' bells for summoning the help.

Coombs Cottage

The Cwms, also known as 'Cooms' or 'Coombs Cottage', lies just beyond the end of the Meadow, reached via a little footbridge over the stream. It was built in 1780, and was a water-powered mill for a time. The mill lane marked on the 1813 map can still be traced all the way from the top of the meadow, along the side of the valley to just behind the building. The house was rebuilt in 1896 in the Victorian style – betrayed by the date plates and the difference in the smooth render on the two-storey part of the building versus the rough walls of the old outbuildings.

A very royal fern
The specimen of *Osmunda regalis* in the garden of Rose Cottage is one of the largest of its kind in the UK. Native to Europe, the royal fern can also be found across Africa and south-west Asia. It evolved over 180 million years ago, before the continents split apart and were still a single super-continent known as 'Gondwanaland' – and has remained virtually unchanged since that time. Our very own plant may be around 400 years old, and comprises over 120 individual crowns with a total circumference of 20ft (6.1m).

Opposite Little Craig-y-Borion farmhouse after its restoration in 2016

Above Rose Cottage, one of three holiday cottages on the estate along with Coombs Cottage and Little Breck

TRAETH
BEACH

CLOGWYNI
CLIFFS

MÔR
SEA

CERIGOS
PEBBLES

FFOSILIAU
FOSSILS

ARFORDIR
COAST

The Wider Estate

The Colby Estate extends out beyond the garden, taking in woodland, farmland and coastal cliffs. It covers more than 364 hectares (900 acres) in total and includes several tenant farms.

Scandal in the community

Census counts show that the larger smallholdings, such as Craig-y-Borion and Little Craig-y-Borion, were run by a series of different families over the centuries. Little is known of their personal histories, but one notable exception is the surviving story on the last use of the *Ceffyl pren* or 'wooden horse' in Amroth in 1852. This was a traditional form of mob justice, to humiliate offenders of morality in the community.

It was reported that an unfaithful husband, 40-year-old Francis Severne, who lived at Craig-y-Borion, was paraded around the parish in derision on the wooden ladder. This was at the request of his wife, after she discovered he had been having an affair with 24-year-old Elizabeth Bowler, the governess at Colby Lodge. The shaming didn't work – the adulterous pair ran away together the next day. They set up home and ran a school together in Australia, where their descendants still live.

From farmland to coastal cliffs

Traditionally, lots of small farms were typical of this area of Wales. But over the years the economic pressures on farming have reduced the number of working farms on the estate to just five. The National Trust works across the estate farmland in a variety of ways, including maintaining paths, bridleways, gates and fences, to restore traditional field hedgerows. Some of the land is grazed by sheep or dairy cows, and a small proportion used to grow fodder or cereal crops.

The estate also includes a stretch of coastline between Amroth and Wiseman's Bridge. It marks the start of the 186-mile long Pembrokeshire Coast Path and is also part of the Wales Coast Path, which runs along the entire Welsh coast. The coastal slope or 'undercliff' along this stretch was created when the old, red, sandstone cliff slumped in places. Over the years various ways of managing the brush and scrub on the clifftop grasslands have been tried and tested, including grazing with ponies, sheep and most recently goats.

Fossils and fast cars

This coastal area supports many different types of wildlife, including birds and insects, but is also important for its geology. It is the most complete section of the middle Westphalian A to Westphalian B – part of the Carboniferous strata in the geological record – in the Western South Wales coalfield. These rocks were laid down around 300 million years ago, at a time when the area was dominated by a large river delta. The many fossils here are almost perfect specimens, and are used to make detailed date correlations with rocks from across the world.

The Colby land also takes in the Knight's Way, an ancient pilgrims' route from Amroth to St David's Cathedral in the northwest of the county. It was created by the Knights Hospitaller, a powerful religious military order similar to the Knights Templar, around the time of the Crusades.

Dotted along this section of Colby are occasional rhododendrons and hydrangeas, probably planted by Miss Mason, who it is said enjoyed being driven along the Way at high speed in one of her fast cars.

Opposite An ancient oak on the borders of the Colby Estate

Top left The Colby Estate extends all the way down to the cliffs at Amroth beach

Top right In the newly planted Coed Melyn (Yellow Wood), the ground under the young trees produces a dazzling yellow carpet of buttercups in spring

To the coast

Follow the woodland paths alongside the Meadow, past The Cwms, and it soon joins the road down to Amroth and the beach – a spectacular stretch of coastline. Large pebbles give way to smooth sand, backed by soaring cliffs and framed by rock formations.

In the late 1800s, iron ore was patch-mined here with men working 50ft (15m) up the cliff face. They would drop the quarried stone down onto the beach, where women and children would separate out the ore. It was then transported by boat or tram to ironworks in Stepaside or Carmarthen. These cliff faces are now nesting sites for sea birds such as fulmars and peregrine falcons. Still visible are the thin seams of coal that Colby and Lord Milford once thought would bring them unimaginable wealth.

Trouble on the shores

Another reminder of the region's mining past can be found near the small slipway at the western end of Amroth beach. In the 1930s, an attempt was made to re-open the Merrixton adit, which used to drain the mine runs from Bedlam Pit and Milford's Kilgetty colliery. Two men took on the task one morning, digging by hand, and retreated back to the beach come noon for lunch. Before they could even sit down, a rumble was heard, followed by an enormous outflow of mud and rock. The spewing torrent went on for hours and the men, although experienced miners, were badly shaken. The idea to re-open the adit was abandoned.

Some years later, in 1943, the beach was used for a military supply exercise, code-named Jantzen, a practice run for the D-Day landings at Normandy. Bulldozers disturbed tonnes of stone to give easy access to the beach, which allowed troops and vehicles to come ashore. Older residents still recall the Meadow at Colby 'full of military vehicles' at the time. During the operation, one of the landing craft got into trouble in the water and was wrecked. It remained there for years before finally sinking out of sight.

Other wartime precautions included laying anti-personnel mines in the field in front of Amroth Castle. On planting them, it was explained that all the mines were connected by wire, to be easily found and removed at a later date. When that time came, the first mine was located, but the connecting wire had rusted away. An officer had to use an old map to try to discover the other 52 devices, but he found only 50. In the intervening years, although the land has been populated at various times by cows and caravans, there were no incidents, so perhaps the original count was wrong. There still remains the possibility, however, that there are two mines left undiscovered.

A forest under the sea

One of the most striking features of Amroth beach can only be seen at low tide – the remains of an ancient woodland from more than 7,000 years ago, before this area was submerged by the sea. This fossilised forest comprises the stumps and fallen trunks and branches of oak, willow and alder, among others. Locals have also found bones and antlers from deer, wild ox and other extinct species over the years. Walking sticks and other items have been made from the wood in the past, but this is now discouraged in hope of preserving the forest for future generations.

Looking after Colby Today

The team at Colby has focused on increasing the habitat and wildlife value of all the land that is managed here, from the woods and meadows to the ponds and streams. This is a central tenet of what the National Trust sees as important for its places: to address the massive loss of wildlife in the UK over the past 40 years.

Creating habitats

At its core, the Trust's conservation strategy is about building overlapping habitats for an array of interdependent species, starting with the smallest at the base of the food chain. Keeping the streams and ponds in the Meadow clear and clean, for instance, attracts a multitude of insects, which in turn attract fish such as trout, which then attract otters.

The new wetland area at the bottom of the Meadow is another case in point. It was created to make a habitat for amphibians such as frogs, which were spawning unsuccessfully in small puddles around the estate. A series of interconnected ponds were dug at various depths to accommodate the variable spring rainfall; now frogs, toads and newts are breeding happily in the area.

These creatures attracted grass snakes. So the team added grass heaps nearby, for the snakes to use as nesting piles to incubate their eggs, and cleared areas for them to bask in the sun in the morning. The area also became a potential place for otters to teach their cubs how to swim (they prefer still, shallow water for this). To encourage them, an artificial holt was built by volunteers and local scout groups. The wetland now provides a home for a huge array of aquatic plants and the insects that depend on them, such as great diving beetles, water scorpions, and many different species of dragonflies and damselflies.

Left The wetland area at the bottom of the Meadow is now the perfect place for otters to teach their cubs how to swim

Above Goldcrests are frequent visitors to the wetland area in winter

Right A dragonfly hunting over the ponds in the Meadow

Below A hart's tongue fern unfurling on the forest floor in the East Wood

Wild woodland

The woods at Colby are home to at least 45 species of breeding birds, including the wood warbler and the pied flycatcher, which are not usually seen in south Pembrokeshire. Oak woodland such as this offers a variety of nesting sites. It also supports a huge amount of invertebrates, which provide food for birds such as nuthatches, goldcrests and treecreepers. The nearby farmland and hedgerows provide homes for large numbers of voles and mice, which make a tasty meal for the garden's birds of prey, including barn and tawny owls, buzzards, red kites, goshawks and sparrowhawks. Purpose-built owl roosts, made or donated by our volunteers, have been incorporated into large old trees and disused outbuildings, restored and re-roofed specifically for this purpose.

The forest floor

Another part of the conservation strategy is leaving deadwood to rot down naturally *in situ*. Standing deadwood is wonderful for boring beetles and creates the perfect roost for some bat species, as well as homes for woodpeckers. Lying deadwood, which absorbs water, is great for fungi, which are essential to the ecosystem. Without fungi, leaf litter, deadwood and other organic matter would pile up to over 60ft (18 m) high in just a few years. By breaking it down, the fungi make nutrients available to nourish other trees and plants. Colby can boast many interesting fungi species, including hoof fungus and King Alfred's cakes, which were both used in times past as tinder to light fires. Chicken of the Woods, a very tasty, edible fungus, can also be found hanging in large yellow masses from the trunks of old trees.

The team at Colby is also helping to prolong the life of some of the older, more important trees in the woodland; by rerouting pathways, taking the strain of constant footfall away from their roots and, in some cases, thinning out the competing trees around them.

Farming for nature

In 2016 the Trust regained about 25 acres of Craig-y-Borion farm. By working closely with neighbouring tenant farmers, the habitat value of the farmland for nature conservation can now be vastly improved.

CYNEFIN
HABITAT

NATUR
NATURE

BLODAU
FLOWERS

TIR FFERM
FARMLAND

PRYFED
INSECTS

GLASWELLTIR
GRASSLAND

Left Barn owls can often be seen hunting on the farmland surrounding Little Craig-y-Borion

Below Path through the newly planted Coed Melyn (Yellow Wood)

Opposite Plans to improve the habitats on the Colby Estate will mean an increase in wildflowers, providing year-around nectar for bees and other insects

Nature's corridors

Many hedgerows across the farmland are being widened into woodland strips, connecting the wooded valleys of Craig-y-Borion to the west and Little Craig-y-Borion to the east. In total, these two wooded valleys already provide 79 hectares (195 acres) of native species woodland. Joining them together with these new 'woodland corridors' will significantly increase the range of the many thousands of plants, bryophytes, fungi, insects, birds and mammals species dependant on native woodland for their habitat. In 2016, just over 3.5 hectares (8 acres) of land were identified across Craig-y-Borion Farm as potentially vulnerable to nirate-rich run-off and soil erosion from any type of intensive farming. This is being turned over to new, more open woodlands made up of clumps of native hazel, blackthorn and hawthorn using trees grown on site, in a nursery created and run by volunteers.

Planning ahead

A series of habitat improvement plans are now going ahead, including the creation of permanent meadows and broadening field margins of wildflower-rich grassland. Some sown with wildflower mixes will provide year-round nectar for pollinating insects, and those sown with wild-seed mixes are designed to provide food for over wintering birds. These experiments are being recorded to see which seed mixes and sowing methods provide the best results. Before they began, a baseline survey of wildlife was undertaken on site. When repeated in several years' time, hopefully it will show a big increase in the numbers and types of species within these habitats. Even with the naked eye, it is already possible to see boosted levels of bird and bee activity in the area.

A Natural Playground

Everything at Colby has been tailored to make sure visitors know they are free to play. There aren't any signs telling you what you can and cannot do; instead, you will find a natural playground with plenty of opportunities to let go and have a good time.

In summer, the stream bounces with flotillas of small, split logs racing to the finish line, shrieked over by children armed with nets and balancing damply on stepping stones. For those feeling brave, the big tree trunk in the Meadow is great for scrabbling on (there are some steps cut in to help get you started). You can teeter across the stream on one of the log bridges or fly high on the rope swing over the water. These structures are regularly tested for safety, but we know that the thrill of a little mild peril is what makes it so exciting in the first place.

Right Borrow one of the pond-dipping kits and explore what lurks in the ponds and stream at Colby

Building a relationship with nature

Children can explore the woods and find secret fairy doors, or hunt out the hidden hedge house. There are definitely no adults allowed in Dylan's den, located in the Meadow's bamboo grove, just south west of the house. It makes the perfect base from which to venture forth to find mini-beasts and bugs, armed with one of the free-to-borrow bug-hunting kits. Or borrow a pond-dipping kit and explore the life in the streams and ponds. Visitors are also welcome to cook on a campfire, build a dam, or make mud pies from the clay of the riverbed.

We believe this is the best way to build a child's relationship with nature – by letting them experience it for themselves, using their imaginations to bring it to life.

Below The rope swing is one of the many opportunities for natural play at Colby

Right Duck racing on the stream

Below right Children (and adults) can test their balancing skills on the log causeway at the top of the West Wood

Colby's Flora

Trees
Coed

Oak Derwen
Ash Onnen
Yew Ywen
Rowan Cerddinen
Hawthorn Draenen wen
Scots pine Ffynidwydden
Giant fir Ffynidwydden lwydlas
Beech Ffawydden
Silver birch Bedwen arian
Alder Gwernen
Elder Ysgawen
Hazel Collen
Wayfaring tree Gwifwrnwydden
Willow Helygen
Poplar Poplysen
Wild cherry Ceiriosen dde
Wild service tree Cerddinen wyllt
Holly Celynnen
Field maple Masarnen fach
European larch
Llawrwydden Ewrop
Coastal redwood
Cochwydden arfor
London plane
Planwydden Llundain
Sweet chestnut
Castanwydden bêr
Horse chestnut
Castanwydden y meirch
Spindle Pisgwydden

Wildflowers
Blodau Gwyllt

Yellow rattle Cribell felen
Meadow buttercup
Crafanc brân y gweunydd
Common nettle Danhadlen
Sweet violet Fioled bêr
Wood sorrel Suran y coed
Cranesbill Pig-yr-Aran
Cuckoo flower Pidyn y gog
Wild carrot Moronen y maes
Heather Grug
Meadowsweet Erwain
Primrose Briallen
Bramble Miaren
Wild strawberry Mefusen wyllt
Clover Meillionen
Great willowherb Helyglys per
Bogbean Ffeuen y gors
Forget-me-not Ysgorpionllys
Bird's foot trefoil Pysen y ceirw
Black medick Maglys gwyneiddu
Comfrey Cyfardwf
Selfheal Y feddyges las
Speedwell Rhwyddlwyn
Thistle Ysgallen
Honeysuckle Gwyddfid
Knapweed Y bengaled
Hawkweed Heboglys

Ferns
Rhedyn

Royal fern Lloerlys
Hart's tongue fern Tafod yr hydd
Polypody Rhedynen y derw
Spleenwort Duegredynen
Adder's tongue Tafod y neidr
Bladder fern Rhedynen godog
Male fern Marchredynen wryw
Shield fern Marchredynen
Hard fern Gwibredynen

Pond Plants
Planhigion Pwll

Pondweed Dyfrllys
Waterweed Ffugalaw
Water plantain Llyriad y dŵr
Arrowhead Saethlys
Water lily Lili'r dŵr
Rush Brwynen
Flag Gellesgen
Duckweed Llinad y dŵr

Grasses
Gweiriau

Sedge Hesgen
Fescue Peisgwellt
Meadowgrass Gweunwellt
Sweetgrass Perwellt
Oatgrass Ceirchwellt
Dog's tail Rhonwellt
Bentgrass Maeswellt
Foxtail Cynffonwellt